SPOTLIGHT
ON CHILDREN'S
AUTHORS

JEFF KINNEY

SUE CORBETT

Cavendish
Square

New York

Published in 2014 by Cavendish Square Publishing, LLC
303 Park Avenue South, Suite 1247, New York, NY 10010

Library of Congress Cataloging-in-Publication Data

Corbett, Sue.
Jeff Kinney / Sue Corbett.
p. cm.—(Spotlight on children's authors)
Summary: "Presents the biography of children's book author Jeff Kinney while exploring his creative process as a writer and artist and the cultural impact of his work"—Provided by publisher.
Includes bibliographical references and index.
ISBN 978-1-60870-932-8 (hardcover)—ISBN 978-1-62712-140-8 (paperback)—ISBN 978-1-60870-939-7 (ebook)
1. Kinney, Jeff—Juvenile literature. 2. Authors, American—21st century—Biography—Juvenile literature.
3. Children's stories—Authorship—Juvenile literature. I. Title. II. Series.
PS3611.I634C68 2013
813'.6—dc23
[B]
2011034036

Senior Editor: Deborah Grahame-Smith
Art Director: Anahid Hamparian
Series Designer: Kay Petronio

Photo research by Lindsay Aveilhe
Cover photo by t14/t14/ZUMA Press/Newscom

The photographs in this book with permission and through courtesy of:
Matt Hoyle Photography: p. 4; Picture Desk: p. 6; Courtesy of Hornbake Library, University of Maryland © January 22, 1992: p. 10; Greg Heffley is TM and © 2009 Jeff Kinney: p. 13; Courtesy of funbrain.com, © 2000 -2011 Pearson Education, Inc. All rights reserved: p. 16; Photo by Sandy Huffaker/Getty Images: p. 18; Tony Cenicola/The New York Time/Redux: p. 20; Matt Hoyle Photography: p. 23; Chad W. Beckerman: p. 26; Ben Hider/Getty Images: p. 27; Carrie Devorah/WENN.com/Newscom: p. 29; Akira Suwa/Philadelphia Inquirer/MCT/Newscom: p. 30; Stew Milne/The New York Times/Redux: p. 33; Photo by John Tlumacki/The Boston Globe via Getty Images: p. 34; Dylan Buyskes/Onion Studio/abimages via AP Images: p. 36; Piotr Redlinski/The New York Times/Redux: p. 38

Printed in the United States of America

CONTENTS

INTRODUCTION:

If at First You Don't Succeed . . .

As a kid growing up near Washington, D.C., Jeff Kinney dreamed of being in the newspaper.

Not on the front page, silly! He wasn't interested in politics.

Jeff wanted to see his name—and his artwork—on the comics page.

The Kinney family got the newspaper every day. "The first thing I would grab was the comics," Jeff remembers. He'd quickly riffle through the pages to find out what kind of trouble Calvin and Hobbes had gotten themselves into, what weird goings-on had occurred in *The Far Side,* and what Opus of *Bloom County* was up to.

That passion paid off. Before he even graduated from college, Jeff's dream had come true. Sort of.

While attending the University of Maryland, he wrote and drew a popular comic strip, titled *Igdoof*, which appeared daily in the *Diamondback*, the campus newspaper. Jeff's classmates told him they enjoyed following the misadventures of Igdoof, a confused freshman; his roommate, Remedial Ralph; and their circle of comically confused friends.

"I was a little bit famous on campus," Jeff says of his days as a student in College Park, Maryland. "It was my first taste of being a public person and of having an identity as a cartoonist. The *Washington Post* and the *Baltimore Sun* both did features on me. I felt like I was on my way to the big time."

And he was.

Only it would take another fifteen years to get there.

Fregley (played by Grayson Russell) shows Greg (Zachary Gordon) and Rowley (Robert Capron) his "secret freckle" in the 2010 film based on the first book in the *Diary of a Wimpy Kid* series.

Chapter 1
GROWING UP

Jeffrey Patrick Kinney was born on February 19, 1971, in Fort Washington, Maryland, a small town hugging the eastern shore of the Potomac River, south of Washington, D.C.

The area is named for its local fort, which was built in 1809 to keep enemies of the still-new nation from reaching the seat of government via the river. There are still cannons standing sentry on the grounds, but the fort is now part of the National Park Service and a popular spot for hiking, picnics, and fishing.

For Jeff, Fort Washington was a nice place to grow up. (Coincidentally, the neighboring town is named Friendly, Maryland.) Jeff's dad worked for the government, and his mom taught preschool. Jeff has an older sister, Ann Marie; an older brother, Scott; and a younger brother, Patrick. Jeff attended St. Mary's School of Piscataway, a Catholic school in Clinton, and graduated from Bishop McNamara High School in Forestville, which did not admit girls until 1992.

Though Jeff calls his childhood "perfectly normal," he admits that he mined his own experiences to create misadventures for Gregory Heffley, the "hero" of his *Diary of a Wimpy Kid* books. Jeff really did once hide from his swim coach in the bathroom, where he wrapped himself with toilet paper, mummy style, to keep down his shivering.

And as he told an audience at the 2009 National Book Festival in Washington, D.C., his high-school athletic career was cut short when he took the soccer coach's directions literally: "My coach said, 'Get your butts over here,' so I ran at him with my butt pointed at him. That was my last day of freshman soccer."

His English teacher, Alfred Odierno, remembers Jeff as a bright and engaged student who "did his share of staring out the window and doodling in his notebook. Jeff was the kind of dreamer every English teacher wants in his class," Odierno recalls. "He often had that look in his eye that he was far away—not zoned out, but dreaming the way the poets tell us to do: 'Hold fast to dreams. . . .' English teachers always remember kids like that."

Odierno suspects that Jeff's artwork was also the way Jeff distinguished himself in a school where athletic ability was highly prized.

ARE YOU FREGLEY?

When a young reader asked Jeff about his inspiration for the character Fregley, Jeff said, "I think most kids have a kid like Fregley on their street, a kid that's a little strange, and if you don't know any kids that are like Fregley, then you might be Fregley."

"In an all-boys school that in those years lived and died by the results of the latest football or basketball game, dreaming doesn't always fit the mold," Odierno said. "But [Jeff] could always draw, and his casual sketching, I suspect often done when he was supposed to being doing something else, was enjoyed by everyone."

Jeff contributed comic strips to the high-school newspaper, the *Stang* (short for *mustang*, the school mascot), but his passion for funny doodling didn't develop in full until he arrived at college. As a freshman at Villanova University, he attended an open-house night for campus activities and approached some students who were looking to recruit newcomers for the newspaper staff.

"I offered to write the crossword puzzle," Jeff said. He was serious, but the newspaper staffers laughed because they thought he was joking. Jeff recovered quickly: "To save face, I said, 'Actually, I want to do a cartoon.' They liked that idea."

That was the beginning of *Igdoof*, a comic strip that appeared first in the weekly newspaper, the *Villanovan*. In a lot of ways, Igdoof is Greg Heffley's ancestor. He's a goofy-looking line drawing whose features— big ears, bulbous nose, bug eyes—are exaggerated for comic effect. Like Greg's, Igdoof's sense of humor is, shall we say, unrefined.

"Igdoof was my alter ego—an extremely awkward freshman bumbling through college," Jeff remembers. Igdoof needed friends, so Jeff gave him an older roommate named Ralph. "It was a sort of Bert and Ernie setup," Jeff said. "There was a lot of tension between the two of them."

After his freshman year, Jeff switched colleges, and Igdoof transferred with him. Jeff convinced the editors at the University of Maryland to run the strip in their daily newspaper, the *Diamondback*. Due to the demands of producing a daily comic strip (rather than a

Igdoof   **Jeff Kinney**

The *Diamondback* ran Jeff's Igdoof comic strip for the first time on January 22, 1992.

weekly one), Jeff switched to a less demanding major—from computer science to criminal justice.

"I was on the verge of flunking out because I was focusing all my attention on *Igdoof*," Jeff admits.

But Jeff did already know a lot about computers. During summers and school vacations, he worked as a programmer for the Bureau of Alcohol, Tobacco, Firearms and Explosives, the federal agency that tracks the illegal use and sale of firearms, explosives, and alcohol and tobacco products. In fact, Jeff might be Agent Kinney today if not for a hiring freeze at the bureau in 1993, the year he graduated from college.

Instead of becoming an agent after college, Jeff worked an additional year at the *Diamondback* before moving to Massachusetts to work as a page designer at the *Newburyport Daily News*, north of Boston. Later he took a job as a computer programmer at a medical software company, but all the while, in his free time, he was pursuing his real goal: becoming a syndicated newspaper cartoonist.

Most newspapers do not have their own cartoonists on staff. Syndicates sell comic strips like *Dilbert, Zits,* and *Doonesbury* to newspapers. A syndicate is a company that represents many artists and typically sells a whole package of features—such as comic strips, puzzles, and horoscopes—to a newspaper or to its parent company. Newspapers may pay very little to run each strip, but if the syndicate sells a comic strip to a lot of newspapers and it is published every day, an artist can earn enough to make a living.

If the comic strip becomes very popular, as *Garfield* by Jim Davis did, the syndicate can demand a higher fee. It can also sell the rights to use images from the strip on merchandise like greeting cards, calendars, and T-shirts. Sometimes, comic-strip characters even walk right out of the newspaper and onto their own TV shows or movies, like Charlie Brown, Lucy, and other characters from Charles Schulz's *Peanuts*.

Getting a syndicate to take on a comic strip is very competitive, however. Each year a syndicate can receive thousands of submissions, and it usually chooses only a few.

When Jeff was pitching his idea in the mid-1990s, the leading syndicates in the United States included King Features, Universal Press, United Media, the Washington Post Writers Group, and Tribune Media Services. But because of dwindling newspaper readership and other factors, fewer newspaper clients were seeking comic strips, especially new strips that didn't already have a following. The market for new comics had never been worse, as Jeff found out when he started sending samples of *Igdoof* to the major syndicates.

"I tried everybody, and I tried them all multiple times," Jeff recalled. "I probably did four or five major submissions over two years, and all I ever got were rejections. I think I got one personal letter from Jay Kennedy at King Features. Everything else was just a form rejection letter."

Jeff felt dejected. He believed his line drawings weren't sophisticated enough for the syndicates. It would have been understandable, after three or four years of trying, to give up at that point. Jeff had landed a good job at FunBrain.com, part of the Family Education Network, where he created interactive online games for a site he started called Poptropica. "We were the number-one kids' website," he said.

It would have been easier to focus on making more online games for an eager audience than to keep writing a comic strip nobody wanted to buy. But one day, on the way home from work, Jeff passed a billboard that featured a quote from Benjamin Franklin.

"Well done is better than well said," it read. For some reason, this sentiment hit Jeff hard. He thought about his artwork and his dream of making a comic strip. If his cartoons weren't good enough to sell to a syndicate, should he just quit? Or should he be working harder to make them better?

"There [are] so many people who tell you what they're going to *do* and then they don't do it," Jeff told *Washington Post* reporter Bob Thompson. "So I was like, 'I'm going to do something and I'm going to keep it really quiet.'"

Jeff bought a sketchbook to record his ideas regularly. His plan was to jot down jokes, drawings, and doodles. He didn't start out thinking he would create a mock journal of a middle-school–age boy, but a lot of what he wound up writing was based on the funny things he remembered from his childhood. And although Jeff got the sketchbook as a way of "shaming myself into . . . writing my comic strips," a funny thing happened as he continued to work on it. Instead of comic strips, what emerged was something that looked more like an illustrated diary. "I would write a little bit and then doodle a drawing in the margins to go with it," Jeff said. "Finally, I realized, 'That's an appealing format.'"

A novel with cartoons? He didn't think that had been done before.

It worked on another level for Jeff, too. Because he didn't have a lot of confidence in his artwork, creating the journal as it if were the work of an actual seventh grader took off some of the pressure; the artwork didn't have to look exceptionally polished or sophisticated. The main character became a rather clueless boy named Greg Heffley, a stick figure with a lollipop head and three untamed hairs sprouting from his scalp.

A quote from Benjamin Franklin inspired Jeff to create his comic antihero.

Jeff thought there might be an audience of grown-ups, like him, who would get a kick out of reading about those comically awkward years between adolescence and adulthood.

He vowed to fill every last page of the sketchbook, a process that took about four years. He then spent another two years refining the artwork and the writing.

By 2004, Jeff had spent almost seven years journaling in the voice of Greg Heffley. He thought he had enough material to create "a big fat book—1,000 pages long," chronicling Greg's ups and (mostly) downs.

What he didn't have was a publisher.

Meanwhile, Jeff continued to work at the Family Education Network. His boss, Jess Brallier, asked him to think about what they could add to FunBrain.com to keep kids visiting the site during the summer months. Many kids access FunBrain.com during school hours, so when school ends for summer vacation, traffic to the site drops.

Jeff told his boss he was working on a book, titled *Diary of a Wimpy Kid,* that was told in journal entries. Perhaps, he wondered, they could serialize the entries from his unpublished journal and post one each day during the summer so kids would want to check in on what Greg Heffley was up to now—just like Jeff had been eager to follow his favorite comics in the newspaper when he was a kid.

"I had been in publishing long enough to know that just about everybody is 'working on a book,'" Brallier said. "So I told Jeff I would look at it, but I also told him, 'If it isn't any good, I'm going to have to tell you that.'"

Jeff didn't have to worry about his boss's reaction for very long. Just a few hours after he sent Brallier the journal, Jeff's phone rang.

"I remember sitting in my kitchen and laughing out loud," Brallier said. "I called him back at eleven o'clock that night, saying, 'Let's publish this online.'"

The first entry in *Diary of a Wimpy Kid* appeared on FunBrain.com on May 8, 2004.

The rest, as they say, is history.

Greg Heffley's journal first appeared in May 2004
as a daily feature on FunBrain.com.

Chapter 2
THE ROAD TO PUBLICATION

Within a few months of posting *Diary of a Wimpy Kid* online, more than 30,000 kids were checking in every day to read Greg Heffley's journal.

Within a year, the number was up to 70,000 visitors daily. "I remember telling people, 'The most read "book" in the world right now is being published on FunBrain.com,'" Jess Brallier said. "Was it on the best-seller list? No. Could you buy it at a bookstore? No. It was free on FunBrain.com."

Jeff posted an entire year of Greg's journal on FunBrain.com before ending the project. (These entries are still available for viewing on the website.) He figured now that he had a polished year in Greg's life, he might be able to find an editor to publish them as a big, thick book. For grown-ups. Like Jeff.

The first place he went to find a publisher was Comic-Con 2006 in New York City.

Comic-Con, which began in California in 1970, is an annual convention that celebrates the contribution of comics to popular art and culture. It's also a big show for introducing new comics-related material. If a company publishes comic books or graphic novels, Comic-Con is where it presents its latest creations, because people who are looking for

Each year, Comic-Con draws thousands of people (a few dressed as superheroes) to its showcase of the latest in comics and graphic novels.

new content for their bookstores, libraries, websites, TV shows, movies, and video games go there to see what's on exhibit.

So Jeff's trip to Comic-Con was, primarily, a shopping expedition to find new material for FunBrain.com and Poptropica. But he tucked a spiral-bound sample of *Diary of a Wimpy Kid* into his briefcase, just in case.

When Jeff arrived at the convention center in New York City, however, he learned that Comic-Con had sold out—there was no way to get in. He might have turned around and gone back to Massachusetts, but he had incentive to stay: tickets to see Billy Joel at Madison Square Garden that night.

So he did what Greg Heffley undoubtedly would have done. He snuck in a side door.

As Jeff strolled the aisles of the convention center and looked at all the displays from companies that published comics, he tried to be cool. He noticed a lot of other people walking around with portfolios and sample comics, and some of their work didn't look so good. He worried that his would look as lame to them as theirs did to him.

Jeff is shy by nature. Pitching his artwork to people he didn't know took courage. He pulled out his sample book only a few times. One publisher laughed when Jeff said he was hoping to create a seven-hundred-page book consisting of illustrated diary entries, many of which had already been published online for free.

He had been hoping for laughs, but not *that* kind of laugh.

Finally, someone mentioned that Abrams ComicArts, a book publisher based in New York City, had recently turned a Web comic, *Mom's Cancer* by Brian Fies, into a book. It was a compilation of comic-strip panels revealing how Fies's family dealt with their mother's critical illness. As Jeff was heading for the exit, he noticed a copy of *Mom's Cancer* on display at the Abrams booth and thought he would risk one last pitch.

"He says I sold him a copy of *Mom's Cancer*, but that part I don't remember," said Charles Kochman, then an editor in Abrams's adult-books division. "I remember everything after that."

Kochman had worked at DC Comics and *Mad* magazine, as well as for a children's book publisher, but Abrams ComicArts did not publish kids' books. (Their affiliated imprint, Amulet Books, did.) Looking back, Jeff thinks he may have lucked into meeting the only person at Comic-Con with the right kind of background to understand *Wimpy Kid*'s potential. He showed Kochman his spiral-bound sample, with its line drawing of Greg on the cover.

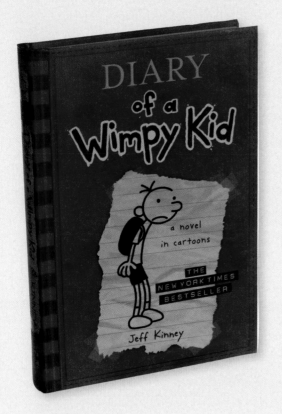

The maroon-colored cover of the first book in the *Wimpy Kid* series was chosen to suggest the paperback edition of another famous first-person story: J.D. Salinger's *Catcher in the Rye.*

"As soon as he said the title, he had me," Kochman recalled. "The eight-year-old inside me totally responded. The mixture of text and pictures gave it the feeling of not being overwhelming; it hit all the right notes. I watched him walk away and I felt, 'This is going to turn into something.'"

Though Kochman's instincts were right, he first had to convince his bosses—and they had doubts.

"People didn't think Greg was a likeable character," Kochman remembered. "They were worried that he never learns anything. All those things were pluses for me, but not everybody was comfortable with that."

No one at the publishing house was sure of what to make of Kinney's big selling point either—that Greg Heffley already had attracted a substantial online fan base. Did that mean people would be willing to pay for a print version—or that nobody would buy it if they could read it free online? They weren't sure.

Finally, someone suggested Kochman see what the children's books division, Amulet Books, thought of *Wimpy Kid*.

The folks at Amulet were interested! But not in a big, thick book. They thought *Wimpy Kid* would be more successful if they broke up Greg's year into installments, maybe three books in a series.

Kochman called Jeff with the good—and bad—news. Yes, Jeff's book was going to be published. But not as he had envisioned it.

"It was kind of a shock to me," Jeff remembers, "because I definitely wrote it with adults in mind. But I quickly got over any feeling of disappointment. I was just excited I was going to be published."

Less than a year later, a box arrived on Jeff's doorstep. Inside were finished copies of his first book, *Diary of a Wimpy Kid*, with the same line drawing of Greg Heffley that had been on the cover of the sample book he had showed Kochman at Comic-Con. "We just added a backpack," Kochman said.

Jeff says that, to this day, the thrill of holding that finished book in his hands is probably the one moment he treasures most about his publishing experience.

"I was just amazed at how nicely it was bound and how professional it looked," Jeff said. "I remember wishing I could just jump into a whole pool filled with copies of my book."

Jeff visited many bookstores to promote his first book.

Chapter 3
BEST-SELLERDOM

To illustrate Amulet Books's expectations for *Diary of a Wimpy Kid*, consider the number of copies it printed for the first edition of the first book in the series.

The first print run, in book publishing, is a carefully calculated figure. Everybody at a company weighs in because the publisher does not want to print more books than it can sell. Sales representatives, who will try to convince bookstores and libraries to stock the book, offer their opinions about how a given title might do. If the editorial department feels very strongly about a particular book, it becomes a "house favorite," one that the editors will passionately talk up to the people they meet at conventions and conferences. Finally, the publisher has to decide how big a risk the company is willing to take. If the book is by a first-time author with no track record, most publishers are cautious. After all, if the book becomes a big hit, more can be printed.

The first printing for book one in the *Diary of a Wimpy Kid* series was 15,000 copies. That was Amulet's best guess about how many books they would sell within a year.

Now consider the first printing for book five in the series: *Diary of a Wimpy Kid: The Ugly Truth*.

The first printing was 5 *million* copies.

Although it didn't take a whole year to sell those first 15,000 copies (Do you have one? It could be worth a lot someday!), Jeff's first book did not arrive with BEST-SELLER stamped all over it.

A year after he first met Jeff, and in time for Comic-Con in February 2007, Kochman had finished copies of *Diary of a Wimpy Kid* to put on display. "Nobody was interested," he remembered.

Jeff says that his first signings at bookstores drew, on average, half a person. "I don't mean there was half a person there—sometimes there would be one, sometimes nobody—so 0.5 on average," he recalls. At one California bookstore, he gave his entire presentation to the only person who showed up: a young girl. "I think it was very awkward for *her*," Jeff said, laughing.

Although there was not a lot of prepublication buzz—the industry term for a book that has all the makings of a best-seller—kids took over the marketing campaign once copies of *Wimpy Kid* actually showed up in bookstores in April 2007.

"Something viral happened," said Kochman. "One kid got hold of the book, and he told his friends, and pretty soon every kid in the class was reading it." On May 6, 2007, less than a month after the book was officially released, it appeared on the *New York Times* best-seller list.

"I can tell you, none of us was expecting that," Kochman said.

Diary of a Wimpy Kid and its sequels went on to dominate the best-seller lists for several years. Jess Brallier, Jeff's boss at the Family Education Network, remembers picking up the *Wall Street Journal* a few years ago. "Four of the five best-selling books were Jeff's," she said. "I've worked with a lot of best-selling authors and there are moments when you know a book is about to take off, and that's very exciting. But no one ever imagined *Wimpy Kid* would explode like this. I have never seen anything like it."

It's not just American kids who love to read Greg's diaries. Amulet reports the series has been translated into thirty-seven languages.

Kochman says that one of the moments when he realized he had unleashed not just a book but a phenomenon was on a cold winter night in January 2009, when he and Jeff traveled to Carle Place, New York, to meet fans and to autograph copies of the third book, *The Last Straw*.

THE WIMPY KID AROUND THE WORLD

The German title of *Diary of a Wimpy Kid*—*Greg's Tagebuch: Von Idioten Umzingelt*—translates to *Greg's Diary: I'm Surrounded by Idiots*. In Brazil, the book is called *Diário de um banana*.

"We had gotten there early and went into a back room to sign the store's stock," Kochman explained. (Authors are often asked to sign a number of books that the store can sell later as autographed copies.) "When Jeff and I came out after a while, the place was packed. There were something like three thousand people there. It was like that scene from *Jaws* when Roy Schneider finally sees the shark and says, 'We're going to need a bigger boat.'"

The store sold every copy it had on hand—about 1,300 books. At the last minute, an Abrams sales manager brought four hundred extra copies to the store in a van.

Jeff's publisher, Amulet Books, has sold almost 50 million copies of books in the *Wimpy Kid* series.

Greg's adventures have moved beyond the printed page—in 2010, he made his big-screen debut. The film, starring newcomers Zachary Gordon (as Greg) and Robert Capron (as Rowley), grossed $75 million at the box office. This ensured demand for the sequel, which was released in March 2011. The sequel was also a success, and the third film in the series was released in August 2012.

Greg also literally left the earth when Macy's commissioned a balloon likeness of the *Wimpy Kid* for its eighty-fourth annual Thanksgiving Day Parade in New York City. At 56 feet (17 meters) tall, weighing 280 pounds (127 kilograms), it was definitely the least wimpy Greg had ever been!

"That was crazy," Jeff recalled. "We were invited to watch them inflate the balloons the night before the parade. It was a really wild moment that hasn't even sunk in yet."

Greg Heffley towers over Manhattan's Sixth Avenue during the eighty-fourth Annual Macy's Thanksgiving Day Parade in November 2010.

To promote the release of the film, Jeff wrote
The Wimpy Kid Movie Diary, released in 2010.

Chapter 4
HOW HE DOES IT

Perhaps the only person who isn't surprised about the *Wimpy Kid* series' phenomenal success is Greg Heffley. After all, on page two of the first book in the series, he writes about his reluctant decision to keep a journal:

> The only reason I agreed to do this at all is because I figure later on when I'm rich and famous, I'll have better things to do than answer people's stupid questions all day long. So this book is gonna come in handy.

Having a lot of things to do is something Jeff can certainly relate to these days. It may have taken him nine years to write the first *Diary of a Wimpy Kid* book and to find a publisher for it, but since 2006, he has written six more novel-length installments, plus Greg's *Movie Diary*, and has acted as executive producer of all three *Wimpy Kid* films, which were shot on location in Vancouver, British Columbia. Just before the release of the second film in March 2011, Jeff estimated he'd made nearly forty trips from Massachusetts to Vancouver on film-related business.

Jeff laughs at the antics of Zachary Gordon and Robert Capron, the stars of the first three *Wimpy Kid* movies.

All this, and Jeff still has his full-time job at the Family Education Network!

"It keeps everything normal to come into the office and be treated as just one of the voices at the conference table," said Jeff's boss, Jess Brallier. "But can you imagine how hilarious it is for me to have to give this guy a performance review?"

It may seem like Jeff is some sort of superhuman, but he says he's not. When someone told him that *Time* magazine had named him one of 2009's Most Influential People, he thought the person was pulling his leg. "I don't even think I'm the most influential person in my own house," he said.

Though he loves what he does, Jeff says it's hard work.

"Both writing and drawing are a struggle for me. I am cursed with being a very slow illustrator, and [each] book requires at least one thousand illustrations," Jeff said in an interview on familyeducation. com. "So sometimes, the joy of illustrating is a bit diminished by the amount of time that illustrating takes. What I enjoy is seeing the words and illustrations come together on the page."

Jeff's process in creating the *Wimpy Kid* books is different from how most writers approach a novel-length work. His first task is to think of as many funny things that can happen to Greg as he possibly can.

"I work very slowly over a number of months, mainly coming up with jokes and then trying to string them together in a narrative," Jeff said. "I like a good story as much as anyone else, but what I'm after is jokes. I'm trying to get a laugh out of the reader on every page. Sometimes I think I'm not writing books as much as joke delivery systems."

Another thing that is different about Jeff is that unlike most other professional illustrators, he has not had any formal training in art. A doodler since grade school, he credits his fifth-grade teacher, Eleanor Norton, with giving him the best advice he ever got.

"I was a pretty good illustrator, and most of my classmates told me they liked my work. But Mrs. Norton pointed out the things I could do better," Jeff said. "She encouraged me to do my very best and to never settle. That's stuck with me."

Before he sold his first book, Jeff worried that his art did not have the "professional veneer" it needed to be successful, but his editor, Charles Kochman, thinks the simplicity of his line drawings is part of the appeal for kids.

"With a lot of illustrators, you really see the hand of the adult in the artwork," Kochman said. "Jeff's art is not as finely rendered, but what I like about that is the adult is almost invisible. It's easy to believe this is Greg's work, not Jeff's, so it's a good match for the text. But it's not easy at all to do that. There's a lot of nuance to what Jeff does."

Though styles vary widely, most of today's working illustrators began honing their craft the same way Jeff did: working with pencil on paper.

Cartooning used to be a lot more tedious than it is today. Now illustrators like Jeff use sophisticated technology to create their work.

Jeff begins each illustration on a Wacom Cintiq drawing tablet, which consists of an LCD screen and a special drawing pen similar to a stylus. Jeff draws directly on the screen, which is attached to his computer. When Jeff draws a circle for Greg's head, it appears instantly on his computer monitor. This is a great time-saving device for artists, who once had to mail drawings to their editors or publisher, who would then have to mail the work back for any corrections or scan it in and send it as an e-mail attachment, losing some quality in the process.

Sitting in his home office in Massachusetts, Jeff shows off the drawing tablet he uses to create the artwork for his books.

Though Jeff writes mostly jokes, one question he gets repeatedly is whether Greg Heffley is based on his own adolescent self. The answer is, not really.

Jeff does have an older brother, Scott, who played in a band while in high school, and a younger brother, Patrick. But Jeff says that Greg, who is always looking for the path of least effort, "is made up of my worst parts and then exaggerated ten times."

Perhaps Jeff gets that question so often because of the diary format of the books. Greg tells his own story, in first person, and his "I" gets blurred with the author creating his voice. And Jeff admits he has reinvented some funny things that happened to him for use in Greg's diaries. Jeff has two young sons, Will and Grant, and he says they also frequently provide him with "comic gold." For instance, his oldest son, Will, is "a mini-Greg Heffley," Jeff told the audience at the 2009 National Book Festival. Will's preschool class would end the day by picking things

Jeff plays with his kids' toys while his younger son, Grant, looks on.

up while singing the "Clean Up" song from the TV show *Barney*. But Will told his parents, "I just sing the song, I don't actually do any of the cleaning up." Jeff also overheard his wife, Julie, asking Will to go outside and ride his bike. Will responded by telling his mother that he was an "indoor person."

Be careful what you say in front of a writer!

Jeff greets Annie Jarvis, whose mom entered a contest and won a "red carpet premiere" of the second Wimpy Kid movie, Rodrick Rules, at Annie's school in Buffalo, New York.

Chapter 5
TO BE CONTINUED . . .

Though Jeff's parents and siblings still live in the Washington, D.C., area, he moved to southern Massachusetts shortly after graduating from college in the mid-1990s. He and his wife and sons live in a small town near the Rhode Island border.

Jeff sometimes goes to the Boston offices of the Family Education Network to work on FunBrain.com or Poptropica, but he can do a lot of work from home, too. Because he was running out of space for his various projects in his family's house, he bought the house next door and turned it into a studio, where he continues to write and draw Greg Heffley's journals and where he works with the executives in charge of the *Wimpy Kid* movies.

"I didn't want to just sell the movie rights and walk away," Jeff said. "I wanted to be as involved as I could be, and it's been a totally different experience. Writing a book is a solo effort. Making a movie is all about collaboration. I have learned a lot."

In fact, Jeff says he's been astounded by all he's learned since he first showed his sample book to Charles Kochman at Comic-Con back in 2006—more than 50 million copies of his books in print, weeks and weeks on the best-seller list, three feature-length films, almost forty foreign-language editions, Greg's appearance in the Macy's Thanksgiving Day Parade—but the thing that has surprised him most, and that has made him happiest, is how his books have been embraced by reluctant readers, especially boys who tell him they don't normally like to read.

"It's impossible not to feel good about that," Jeff said. "If that was all I had ever done, I would still feel like I had accomplished something."

Jeff's editor, Charles Kochman, says he believes part of *Wimpy Kid*'s phenomenal success stems from Jeff's consistent focus on what's best for his young readers.

"I can't tell you how many conversations we've had, and his decision-making is 100 percent, without fail, about how whatever we're doing is going to affect the kids who read his books," Kochman said.

These brothers in Brooklyn, New York, are big fans of Greg Heffley's diaries.

JEFF LIKES TO READ:

Growing up in Maryland, Jeff was an avid reader of the comics page of the *Washington Post*. Here were his favorite comic strips:

Bloom County by Berkeley Breathed

Calvin and Hobbes by Bill Watterson

The Far Side by Gary Larson

He also remembers some favorite books that are probably in your school library:

Freckle Juice by Judy Blume

The Hobbit by J. R. R. Tolkien

Ramona by Beverly Cleary

Tales of a Fourth Grade Nothing by Judy Blume

The *Xanth* series by Piers Anthony

BOOKS BY JEFF KINNEY

Diary of a Wimpy Kid (Amulet, 2007)

Diary of a Wimpy Kid: Roderick Rules (Amulet, 2008)

Diary of a Wimpy Kid Do-It-Yourself Book (Amulet, 2008)

Diary of a Wimpy Kid: The Last Straw (Amulet, 2009)

Diary of a Wimpy Kid: Dog Days (Amulet, 2009)

The Wimpy Kid Movie Diary: How Greg Heffley Went Hollywood (Amulet, 2010)

Diary of a Wimpy Kid: The Ugly Truth (Amulet, 2010)

Diary of a Wimpy Kid: Cabin Fever (Amulet, 2011)

Diary of a Wimpy Kid: The Third Wheel (Amulet, 2012)

GLOSSARY

buzz—Industry enthusiasm that creates excitement for a forthcoming book.

editorial—Related to editors and their work in a publishing company.

executive producer—The person who is in charge of the overall production of a film but usually is not involved in the technical aspects of filmmaking.

imprint—A specific editorial branch of a publisher, shown (imprinted) on the spine of the book and at the bottom of the title page. A publisher may have many imprints, each with its own special focus.

performance review—The process by which a manager examines and evaluates an employee's work.

portfolios—Large, flat portable cases for holding artwork.

print run—The number of books printed at a given time.

remedial—A designation for a course aimed at helping a student to overcome learning difficulties.

sequel—The next installment that continues the story begun in an earlier work.

serialize—To publish or broadcast a story, comic strip, or play in regular installments.

software—The programs and other operating information used by a computer.

syndicate—A company that acquires and distributes material to publish simultaneously in multiple newspapers.

traffic—The number of visitors and visits a website receives.

veneer—An attractive but superficial coating given to an object or a work.

viral—Becoming well known, often on the Internet, because word has circulated rapidly.

CHRONOLOGY

February 19, 1971: Jeff is born in Fort Washington, Maryland.

1989: Jeff graduates from Bishop McNamara High School, Forestville, Maryland.

1993: Jeff graduates from the University of Maryland, College Park, with a degree in criminal justice.

February 2006: Jeff meets editor Charles Kochman, who agrees to take a look at a sample of Jeff's book, *Diary of a Wimpy Kid.*

April 2007: *Diary of a Wimpy Kid* is released by Amulet, an imprint of Harry N. Abrams.

May 2007: *Diary of a Wimpy Kid* appears on the *New York Times* best-seller list for the first time and remains on the list for thirty-nine consecutive weeks.

February 2008: The release of *Diary of a Wimpy Kid: Roderick Rules* takes over the number-one spot on the *Times* best-seller list, bumping the first book down to number two.

January 2009: *Diary of a Wimpy Kid: The Last Straw* is released.

December 2009: Jeff is named one of *Time* magazine's 100 Most Influential People.

March 2010: The film version of *Diary of a Wimpy Kid*, starring Zachary Gordon, debuts in theaters.

March 2011: *Diary of a Wimpy Kid: Roderick Rules* debuts in theaters.

May 2012: Jeff wins Author of the Year at the 2012 Children's Choice Book Awards.

August 2012: *Diary of a Wimpy Kid: Dog Days* debuts in theaters.

FURTHER INFORMATION

Book

Are you interested in trying to write stories yourself? These two books offer guidance:

Levine, Gail Carson. *Writing Magic*. New York: Collins, 2006.

Messner, Kate. *Real Revision: Authors' Strategies to Share with Student Writers*. Portland, ME: Stenhouse, 2011.

Website

www.wimpykid.com

A year's worth of entries in Greg Heffley's journal can be found at www.funbrain.com

BIBLIOGRAPHY

A note to report writers from Sue Corbett

To write this biography, I read all of Jeff's wonderful books and did extensive research online, including reading all the articles that other journalists have written about him. I had interviewed Jeff myself years ago, in my role as the children's book reviewer for the *Miami Herald,* but after I had compiled of list of questions that my research hadn't answered, I interviewed Jeff again. I also spoke to his editor, Charles Kochman; his boss at the Family Education Network, Jess Brallier; former classmates and teachers; booksellers; and librarians.

Following is a list of sources I used to write this biography. Any time *you* write a report, you should also keep track of where you got your information. It is fine to use information that you found somewhere else in your report, as long as you say where you got the information and give the source credit in a footnote or an endnote, or within the report itself. (Your teacher can tell you how he or she prefers you to list your sources.)

It is not fine to pass off other people's work as your own, as Greg Heffley finds out when he tries to pass off Roderick's old history paper as his own. Greg gets an F.

PRINT ARTICLES

"Hapless Boy Wins Eager Friends," by Jan Hoffman. *New York Times*, Jan. 11, 2009.

"An Interview with Jeff Kinney." No author given. Family Education Network. Available at http://school.familyeducation.com/authors/artists/38386.html.

"Get Out of Here! Jeff Kinney Isn't Kidding About How 'Wimpy Kid' Came to Life," by Bob Thompson. *Washington Post*, March 3, 2009.

"The Man Who Made Being Wimpy Cool," by Laura Meade Kirk, *Providence Journal*, March 30, 2008.

"Turns Out 'Wimpy Kid' Is the Popular One," by Sue Corbett, *Miami Herald*, Nov. 15, 2008.

INTERVIEWS

Telephone interview with Jeff Kinney, conducted by Sue Corbett, Feb. 14, 2011.

Telephone interview with Charles Kochman, editor, Amulet Books for Young Readers, conducted by Sue Corbett, Feb. 16, 2011.

Telephone interview with Jess T. Brallier, Family Education Network, conducted by Sue Corbett, February 25, 2011.

ONLINE AUDIO

Interview with Jeff Kinney, conducted by Andrea Seabrook, *All Things Considered*, National Public Radio, Feb. 2, 2008. Available at www.npr.org/templates/story/story.php?storyId=18591415.

INDEX

ABOUT THE AUTHOR:

Sue Corbett is a reporter who has worked for the *Miami Herald*, *People* magazine, and *Publishers Weekly*. She is also the author of several novels for kids, including *The Last Newspaper Boy in America*, *Free Baseball*, and *12 Again*.